Salvation
The Boundless Love of God

Written by
Marion P. McKenzie

Table of Contents

DEDICATION

To my Lord and Savior, Jesus Christ, whose sacrifice is the sole foundation of my freedom and whose grace is the mighty force that has continually catapulted my life.

And to the enduring faith of my Parents, whose healing became a profound demonstration of the Holy Spirit's power and whose life taught me the transformation of prayer.

ACKNOWLEDGEMENT

No journey is taken alone, and I could not have reached this moment without the foundation of love and faith provided by those around me. This book, and the journey it describes, stands on the shoulders of their consistent support.

To my Parents, Eli and Irine James:

I owe an immeasurable debt to you. You first trained me in the way of the Lord, ensuring that the church was a central part of my life every single Sunday. Your discipline became my direction, setting the course for my lifelong walk with God.

To my Siblings, Samuel James (now a dedicated Pastor), Paul, Clarrisa, and Fadia:

You were my first community and my "home choir." I look back with such fondness on the times we spent singing, praying, and reading the scriptures together within the walls of our childhood home.

To my Husband, Roy:

Thank you for being my steadfast partner on this journey of life. I am grateful for your constant encouragement and your readiness to sit with me and study the Word of God. You help keep my feet grounded in faith and truth.

To my Children's:

Kurt, Dwight, Andrew, and Aldene. You have been the great encouragement of my life. You are my greatest blessings.

To my Church Family:

I extend my heartfelt thanks for your spiritual nourishment and community.

To my Pastors. Walker, Marjory, Allan, Minister Bob, David, Whittaker, and Fernandez:

I am grateful for your refreshing sermons that consistently feed my spirit on Sundays.

To Sis Rose and Lisa:

Thank you for interceding on my behalf and lifting me up in prayer, for a truly effective prayer life is always supported by the community of believers.

ABOUT THE BOOK

Salvation by God's Grace is a book that aims to illuminate the central truth of the Christian faith: **The Plan of Salvation**. It is written to serve as a conversation between the author and the reader, a shared journey through ideas and revelation.

The book breaks down salvation into a dynamic reality with three distinct dimensions:

Justification:

The Past Verdict where the believer is declared righteous through faith in Jesus Christ, removing the penalty of sin.

Sanctification:

The Present Process of becoming holy through the continuous work of the Holy Spirit, transforming the believer to be more like Christ.

Glorification:

The Future Promise of complete perfection when the believer is finally delivered from the very presence of sin.

The book also explores the Workable Plan of Inner Transformation through concepts like Regeneration (the new spiritual birth) and Redemption (the price paid for freedom). It then simplifies the path to faith using The Four Spiritual Laws.

Ultimately, the entire Plan is rooted in grace, which is unmerited favor. The book concludes with the author's personal testimony, demonstrating how this divine grace transformed a life from overcoming struggles with childhood devotion to witness the miraculous healing of a mother.

Chapter 1:
The Call to Redemption

1.1 The Universal Search for Meaning

Every human heart, regardless of culture, time, or circumstance, carries within it a profound, restless yearning. This is the **universal search for meaning**. We instinctively know there must be something more, a grand design, a purpose far greater than the routine of our daily lives. We chase fulfilment through career, relationships, achievement, or possessions, yet so often, that sense of completeness remains elusive, like a ghost just beyond our grasp. The deepest desire of the soul is to be connected to the Source of all meaning, to understand our origin, and to grasp our eternal destiny.

This book is a journey into the answer to that longing. It is a detailed exploration of the **Plan of Salvation**, the central theme that binds the entire Christian narrative together, revealing the immense love and meticulous provision of God for humankind.

1.1.1 The Great Divide: Humanity's Need

Why do we need a Plan of Salvation at all? To answer this, we must first recognize the fundamental reality described in the Bible: a great chasm exists between a perfectly holy God and imperfect humanity. The Bible states clearly in Romans 3:23, "For all have sinned and fall short of the glory of God." This isn't a judgment against external bad behavior alone; it's a statement about our intrinsic nature. Sin often defined simply as "missing the mark" is the spiritual default that separates us from a relationship with our Creator. It is the fundamental breakdown that taints our best efforts and blocks the path to true purpose.

This separation is not God's desired state for us. On the contrary, the entire scriptural record, from Genesis to Revelation, is a passionate love letter demonstrating God's relentless movement toward reconciliation. The Plan of Salvation is His ultimate, unchangeable, and compassionate provision to bridge that chasm. It is the definitive declaration of **God's love and compassion** toward man, a magnificent drama played out for our redemption.

1.1.2 The Purpose of This Book: Illumination and Invitation

My primary purpose in writing this book is to **enlighten and inspire** you, the reader, on the Plan of Salvation. It is not merely a theological checklist, but a living, breathing reality that transforms every aspect of life.

This book shows not only *what* God did to save us, but *how* that salvation works in our lives today in the past, present, and future.

We will move beyond simple definitions to explore the **Workable Plan of Salvation**, delving into profound concepts like:

- **Justification:** The declaration of our righteousness.

- **Regeneration:** The moment of new spiritual birth.
- **Redemption:** The price paid for our freedom.
- **Sanctification:** The ongoing process of becoming holy.

These concepts are not dry academic theories; they are the gears and levers of your spiritual transformation. They represent God's promise to deliver us not only from the penalty of sin but also from its present power.

1.1.3 The Foundation of Grace

Ultimately, the Plan of Salvation is entirely rooted in one concept: **grace**. Grace is unmerited Favor, receiving a gift we could never earn and certainly do not deserve. It is the ultimate expression of St. John 3:16: "For God so loved the world that he gave his one and only Son, that whoever believes in him shall not perish but have eternal life."

This book will demonstrate that salvation is an available gift of grace, received through **faith in Jesus Christ**, not through our personal works, achievements, or relentless striving. It is finished work, offered freely. My hope is that by the end of this journey, you will not only understand the Plan of Salvation with greater clarity but also feel its beautiful, life-altering power with greater conviction. Let us begin this exploration of the most important truth ever revealed to humanity.

Chapter 2:
Defining Salvation: Past, Present, and Future

2.1 Salvation: More Than a Moment

If the Plan of Salvation is the central theme of God's interaction with humanity, it is vital to have a comprehensive understanding of what salvation truly is. At its core, **Salvation is deliverance** from the penalty, power, and eventual presence of sin. It is the act of God, rooted in His boundless love, by which He reconciles us to Himself. It is not something we earn through religious effort; it is a gift of grace received through faith in Jesus Christ alone.

This gift, however, is not a static, one-time transaction. The esteemed theologian Earl D. Radmacher articulated salvation as a dynamic reality with three distinct dimensions **Past, Present, and Future** encompassing Justification, Sanctification, and Glorification. Understanding these three facets transforms the Christian life from a single event into a profound, lifelong journey of transformation.

2.2 Justification: The Past Verdict (Declared Righteous)

The first dimension of salvation is **Justification**. This is the **past-tense experience** of salvation, happening the moment an individual places their faith in Jesus Christ.

Imagine a courtroom scene. We stand as the accused, guilty of the charge of sin, which carries the penalty of spiritual death. However, when we accept Christ's sacrifice, a dramatic scene unfolds: Christ steps forward and takes our penalty, and his perfect righteousness is applied to our record. Justification, therefore, is not about *us* becoming perfectly righteous in that instant; it is God **declaring** us righteous. It is a legal, forensic act.

The guilt is removed, the debt is paid, and the separation is nullified. Paul affirms this astonishing truth in Romans 5:1: "Therefore, since we have been justified through faith, we have peace with God through our Lord Jesus Christ." We are completely forgiven of all past, present, and future sins, and we are reconciled.

This dimension is *finished*. It is the bedrock of our security in God.

2.3 Sanctification: The Present Process (Becoming Holy)

The second dimension is **Sanctification**, the **present-tense experience** of salvation. If justification is a legal declaration, sanctification is the practical, **ongoing process** of spiritual growth and transformation.

The moment we are justified, we are *set apart* for God (positional sanctification). But the journey doesn't end there. Sanctification is the work of the Holy Spirit in the believer's life, transforming us from the inside out to become more and more like Jesus Christ. It involves the struggle between our old sinful nature and the new spiritual life we received through Christ.

A sanctified life, as the theologian James Kennedy described, is a life where those who are "effectually called and regenerated... are further sanctified through the virtue of Christ's death and resurrection by His Words and spirit dwelling in them." It is a slow, progressive peeling away of selfish and carnal ways, replacing them with the fruit of the Spirit: love, joy, peace, patience, kindness, goodness, faithfulness, gentleness, and self-control. It is a daily yielding of our will to the guidance of the Spirit, making us progressively **holy** set apart for God's purposes. This dimension is *continuing*.

2.4 Glorification: The Future Promise (Complete Perfection)

The final dimension is **Glorification**, the **future-tense experience** of salvation. This is the grand and certain hope toward which every believer moves. Glorification occurs when we finally enter God's presence, often referred to as the resurrection.

This is the ultimate fulfilment where we are completely delivered from the very *presence* of sin. We will receive a resurrected, perfected body, and our souls will be made perfect, fully reflecting the glory of Christ without stain, blemish, or brokenness. Romans 8:30 beautifully summarizes this trajectory: "And those he predestined, he also called; those he called, he also justified; those he justified, he also glorified." Glorification is God's promise to finish the work He started in us. It ensures that the momentary struggle of sanctification will yield eternal perfection. This dimension is *certain*.

2.5 Understanding the Full Scope of God's Work

To grasp salvation fully is to see it in its majestic entirety: **Justification** provides the peace and reconciliation needed for eternal security; **Sanctification** provides the power and growth needed for holy living; and **Glorification** provides the fulfillment and perfection of the divine intention. Salvation is not a brief stop on the way to heaven; it is the comprehensive work of God to fully redeem, restore, and rewrite the destiny of His beloved children.

Chapter 3:
The Workable Plan: Inner Transformation

3.1 Regeneration: The Moment of New Birth

When a person accepts the gift of justification, an immediate and profound internal miracle must take place to enable them to live the life God has declared them righteous to live. This miracle is **Regeneration**, what the Bible calls the **"new birth."**

Jesus himself told Nicodemus, "Very truly I tell you, no one can see the kingdom of God unless they are born again" (John 3:3). Regeneration is the supernatural act of the Holy Spirit imparting spiritual life to a soul that was once spiritually dead. It's a radical, decisive change where the old self, the one ruled by sin and spiritual blindness, is fundamentally overhauled.

Think of it as a second genesis. The old, spiritual engine that was broken and unresponsive to God is replaced with a new heart and a new spirit, as promised in the Old Testament prophecy (Ezekiel 36:26-27). This transformation is not a self-help regimen; it is a divine creation, making the believer a "new creation" (2 Corinthians 5:17). We are given the capacity to understand spiritual truth, to desire holiness, and to pursue God.

This is why, as Romans 8:13 indicates, the believer can now "live after the Spirit." The Spirit of God now dwells within, providing the power to overcome the desires of the flesh. Regeneration is the indispensable foundation that makes sanctification (the process of holiness) possible. Without this inner life force, any attempt at righteous living is merely external performance.

3.2 Redemption: The Price Paid for Freedom

Hand-in-hand with regeneration is the concept of **Redemption**. If regeneration is the impartation of a new *life*, redemption is the payment that secured our *release* from captivity. The ancient world understood redemption (or *agorazo*) as the act of a buyer going to the market and purchasing a freedom. Humanity, having fallen into sin, was not just guilty (solved by justification) but was also in **bondage to the power and consequences of sin** (solved by redemption). We were slaves to our own fallen nature and destined for eternal consequences.

The necessary price to free us from this cosmic captivity was infinite. The price paid was the precious blood and the very life of Jesus Christ. As the Apostle Paul reminded the elders in Acts 20:28, the church of God was "purchased with His own blood." It was a deliberate, costly transaction.

3.3 *The Significance of the Ransom*

The core meaning of redemption centers on the exchange: our bondage for His sacrifice.

1. **Freedom from Guilt:** Through the ransom, we are released from the debt we owed, freeing us from the conscience-crippling guilt of past mistakes.

2. **Freedom from the Power of Sin:** When we are redeemed, we are no longer compelled to obey sin's demands. While the struggle remains (sanctification), the chains are broken (redemption). The redeemed are given the capacity to say **no** to temptation and **yes** to God's will.

3. **Restoration of Relationship:** Redemption is the path back to fellowship. Ephesians 1:7 confirms this: "In him we have **redemption through his blood**, the forgiveness of sins, in accordance with the riches of God's grace."

Therefore, the Workable Plan of Salvation is a dynamic duo: **Regeneration** gives us the inner capacity to live a new life, and **Redemption** provides the external, costly, and complete release from the past bondage that held us captive. Together, they form the foundation of our existence as children of God, allowing us to walk in the freedom Christ secured.

Chapter 4:
The Four Spiritual Laws: A Simple Path to God

4.1 A Universal Blueprint for Faith

The great truths of the Plan of Salvation Justification, Regeneration, and Redemption are glorious but can sometimes feel complex. To make this ultimate truth accessible and understandable to everyone, the Christian framework often distils the path to faith into four simple, clear steps. These are known as **The Four Spiritual Laws**, a framework popularized by Bill Bright, designed to be a universal blueprint for returning to God.

These four laws systematically address the core components of the human condition and God's provision, guiding the seeker toward a clear decision.

4.1.1 Law 1: God Loves You and Has a Wonderful Plan for Your Life

The journey always begins with the character of God. The first law establishes the foundational, incredible truth: **God loves us and offers a wonderful plan for our lives.**

This is not a theoretical love; it is an active, demonstrating love. The most famous verse in the Bible, John 3:16, is the ultimate proof: "For God so loved the world that he gave his one and only Son, that whoever believes in him shall not perish but have eternal life." This love is the *motive* for the entire Plan of Salvation. It affirms that God's intention for us is never harm or abandonment, but a life of purpose, joy, and eternal security. The wonderful plan is simple: relationship with Him.

4.1.2 Law 2: Humanity Is Separated by Sin

If God's intention is a wonderful relationship, why is it not the universal human experience? The second law addresses the single greatest obstacle: **Humanity is sinful and separated from God.**

Our sinful nature creates an unbridgeable gap between us and a holy God. Romans 3:23 starkly confirms this reality: "For all have sinned and fall short of the glory of God." This gap is spiritual, rendering us incapable of reaching God through our own efforts, good deeds, or religious rituals.

This law is crucial because it helps us abandon the delusion of self-sufficiency. It forces us to acknowledge that we are not just flawed people making mistakes; we are fundamentally disconnected, and we cannot know or experience God's wonderful plan for our lives while this separation exists.

4.1.3 Law 3: Jesus Christ is God's Only Provision

If we cannot reach God, then God must reach us. The third law reveals the sole bridge across the gap of sin: **Jesus Christ is God's only provision for man's sin.** The chasm requires an infinite payment, and only the spotless Son of God could pay it. Romans 5:8 is the triumphant answer to the dilemma of sin: "But God demonstrates his own love for us in this: While we were still sinners, Christ died for us." Jesus is the living, breathing manifestation of God's provision. His death on the cross was the perfect, once-for-all sacrifice that satisfied the requirement for holiness and simultaneously expressed boundless love. There is no other name, no other philosophy, and no other way by which we can be reconciled.

4.1.4 Law 4: We Must Individually Receive Jesus

Understanding the first three laws is necessary, but not sufficient. Intellectual agreement is not the same as transformation. The fourth law requires an active, personal response: **We must individually receive Jesus as our Savior and Lord.**

Salvation is a gift, and a gift is only effective when it is personally accepted. This involves two actions: **Repentance** (turning away from sin) and **Faith** (turning toward Jesus). It is a conscious, decisive commitment to trust.

When we receive Him, we move from being separated individuals to being **children of God**. John 1:12 promises this power and identity: "Yet to all who received him, to those who believed in his name, he gave the right to become children of God." Only then can we truly know and experience the wonderful plan God has for our lives, initiating the magnificent journey of justification, regeneration, and sanctification.

Chapter 5
My Personal Testimony: A Life Catapulted by Grace

5.1 The Second of Seven: Early Lessons in Chores

Having accepted the gift of salvation at a young age, maybe around twelve years old, was the best choice I have ever made in my life. I am a child of God, redeemed by the blood of Jesus, and that foundational truth sustained me through what were sometimes sad and challenging experiences.

I was the second of seven children, and though we were brought up in a Christian home, I often felt burdened by excessive chores. This feeling left indelible marks on my mind. I would sometimes hide under tables or run to my aunt's house to escape, only to be found and returned to face a loving but strict mother. My ultimate judge, my dad, would always ask if I was guilty, and when I denied it, he took my word. These moments of tension, however, never led to hatred, because even then, I knew God lived in me, and as a child, I could not understand rudeness to my parents. I was naive and innocent.

5.2 The Voice in the Chores: Divine Guidance in the Mundane

One vivid experience of **God's mighty deliverance** occurred right in the midst of the mundane. I was washing a mountain of dishes, it felt as though I was partially covered with them when the Holy Spirit showed up and spoke to me. It was the clear, gentle voice of a teacher and a friend.

He said, "When you do your chores, do something for yourself."

I was confused and asked for an explanation. He told me that as I washed the utensils, I could open my class reader, or a mathematics textbook, and read it or solve problems little by little, a glance now and then. This was a profound revelation! Immediately, I put it into practice. As my hands worked through the washing clothes, washing dishes, cleaning the floor, and cooking dinner, my brain engaged in study. I loved it. I had no excuses for not completing my homework and found a secret joy in multitasking, turning a necessary burden into an opportunity for growth.

5.3 *The Secret Command: Achieving Excellence*

This divine guidance continued with a weighty command: The Holy Spirit told me I **must achieve excellence in school** because my siblings, when they became adults, would not have time for me; they would forget about me.

I listened. I followed this instruction secretly and with diligence. God's grace and mercies truly **catapulted my life** in ways that even I could not always understand. The diligence brought about by that secret obedience made me wonder about my family and neighbors. I went from feeling like a child destined for service to realizing I possessed a unique destiny guided by a loving God.

5.4 The Moment of Crisis: A Mother's Healing

The most powerful demonstration of God's grace occurred later, when I was a young adult, married with four children. My mother suffered a bad stroke; she couldn't talk or walk. Seeing her in that state was a terrible shock that left me trembling, gripping my own baby tighter to my chest. I cried quietly and desperately.

Then, my mom spoke, her voice strained, "Could you pray for me please?"

I was terrified. I felt so nervous because, in that moment, I honestly felt I needed prayer myself. Hesitantly, I held her hand and asked the Holy Spirit to help me pray. I opened my mouth and asked God to touch and heal her. As I prayed, my speech sounded like it was transitioning into another language. I paused three times, utterly overwhelmed, but slowly brought the prayer to an end.

Suddenly, the atmosphere in the room shifted. It became light with a beautiful sense of **joy and peace**. I received an absolute inner certainty that my mother would be revived soon.

5.5 From Fear to Faith: The Transformation of Prayer

A few days later, when I went to see her, she was healed and walking around! The first thing she asked me to do was to accompany her to pray for other sick people. While I was happy to see her healing, I did not like the invitation I didn't know much about the power and importance of prayer then, and I certainly didn't feel qualified to be minister.

But that moment marked a critical turning point. The Holy Spirit had used my utter desperation to demonstrate His power through me. I didn't know how to pray, but He provided the language and the power. I now know better. I love praying for others, using my voice and faith as my **Savior and Lord** intended, bringing glory to His precious name.

5.6 *The Enduring Gift: Choosing Grace*

I have grown, little by little, grace by grace. I have been transformed from my selfish and carnal ways into the path of holiness that God requires. My entire life, from the hidden struggles of my childhood to the sudden, miraculous healing of my mother, is a testament to the comprehensive work of the Plan of Salvation. It is not just doctrine; it is destiny. Accepting this gift of grace remains the defining and best choice of my life.

5.7 A Son's Wisdom

Throughout my travels and my walk with the Lord, I have learned that wisdom can come from anywhere, often from those closest to our hearts. One of my children, once shared a profound truth with me that cut through the noise of religious perfectionism. It is a reminder for anyone feeling too broken or "messy" to approach the Throne of Grace.

He reminded me that we do not have to be perfect. In fact, none of us are. Too often, we believe we must clean up our lives before we can walk through the church doors. We think we must conquer our darkest struggles lust, pornography, or intimacy issues on our own strength before we are worthy of God's attention. But as Andrew wrote, "That is a lie from the enemy."

The enemy wants us to hesitate. He wants us to hide in shame. But the invitation of Christ is different. His invitation is simple: Come as you are.

You do not need to fix yourself first. You only need to get to know Jesus, and He will do the changing. The transformation is His work, not a prerequisite for His love. All you have to do is say "Yes." Tell Him, "Lord, I am here simply because You called me."

Faith is not a solitary struggle. It involves talking to a brother or sister in Christ, finding accountability, and letting the community of believers support you. If you can take that small step showing up just as you are that is all it takes for God to start His miraculous work in you.

5.8 Hidden Depths

As I looked out into the deep blue, I was absolutely amazed at the beauty of the "underworld." It was a landscape that mirrored the earth above, yet it held a magic entirely its own. There were formations that looked like hills, pathways that resembled roads, and coral structures standing tall like mountains and trees. But here, instead of birds in the branches, there were myriads of fish and sea creatures gliding through the currents.

The experience was so breathtaking that I couldn't keep it to myself. I remember inviting a group of children to accompany me on a subsequent trip so they, too, could witness the majesty of God's creation beneath the waves.

It is funny how people perceive us. Occasionally, I hear others boasting about their travels or discussing the technicalities of a submarine ride. When I join in the conversation to share my own story, the mood often shifts. They look at me with skepticism, behaving as if someone like me perhaps because of my age or my demeanor could not possibly have been inside a submarine. Their doubt used to bother me, but now I smile. I know the truth. I did it. It is a precious memory I possess, a testament to a life lived fully, and no one can take that away from me. It was God's blessing at work, allowing me to see the depths of His world.

Chapter 6:
The Divine Verdict Foundational Scriptures of Salvation

The Plan of Salvation, which transforms our destiny and catapults our lives, is not based on abstract theory but on concrete, timeless promises found within God's Word. This chapter serves as a powerful compilation of the foundational Scriptures that provide the ultimate authority and assurance for our faith journey, reinforcing the truths of Justification, Redemption, and Glorification.

6.1 The Source of Salvation: Love, Grace, and Provision

Salvation begins and ends with the gracious character of God. The **motive** is His unparalleled love, the **method** is His free gift, and the **scope** is exclusively through His Son.

The foundation is laid in **St. John 3:16**: 'For God so loved the world that he gave his one and only Son, that whoever believes in him shall not perish but have everlasting life.' This verse illuminates the sacrificial core of God's plan, showing that His gift ensures our eternal existence. This gift is received not by effort, but by grace, as confirmed in **Ephesians 2:8-9**: 'For it is by grace you have been saved through faith and that not of yourself: it is the gift of God: not of works lest any man should boast.' Grace is the unmerited favor, the core concept upon which the entire Plan is rooted.

Before receiving this gift, we must first recognize the **necessity** of salvation. **Romans 6:23** clearly defines the great divide and the consequence of sin: 'For the wages of sin is death but the gift of God is eternal life in Christ Jesus our Lord.' The gift is offered through one, and only one, mediator. **Acts 4:12** declares the absolute exclusivity of Christ: "Salvation is found in no other, for there is no other name under heaven given to mankind by which we must be saved."

6.2 *The Mechanism of Reception: Confession and Trust*

The Plan of Salvation requires a decisive, personal response to God's invitation.

The process of receiving Jesus as Savior and Lord is detailed in **Romans 10:9-10**: 'That if you shall confess with your mouth the Lord Jesus and shall believe in your heart that God raised him from the dead, you shall be saved. For with the heart man believeth unto righteousness; and with the mouth confession is made unto salvation.' This highlights that faith is a **heartfelt belief** that leads to **Justification** (declared righteous) and an **outward confession** that confirms **salvation**.

6.3 The Price and the Promise: Redemption and New Identity

Once received through faith, the salvation purchased for us is seen in the concept of **Redemption** (the price paid for freedom).

The incomparable price paid by Christ is explained in **1 Peter 1:18-20**: 'Forasmuch as you know we were not redeemed by corruptible things, as silver and gold... but with the precious blood of Christ, as of a lamb without blemish and without spot, who was ordained before the foundation of the world, but was manifest in this last time for you.' This sacrifice secured the ultimate release from the debt we owed. **Ephesians 1:7** summarizes the result: 'In him we have redemption through his blood, the forgiveness of sins, according to the richness of his grace.'

The results of this redemption are immediate and eternal:

- **Forgiveness and Peace (Justification): Romans 4:7** assures us of the profound peace achieved through faith: 'Blessed are they whose iniquities are forgiven and whose sins are covered.'

- **Adoption (New Birth/Regeneration): St. John 1:12** confirms the new identity we receive upon believing: 'As many as received him, to them he gave the right to become children of God, even to those who believe in his name.' This is the transformation from a separated individual to a child of God.

- **Fellowship and Glory (Glorification):** The Plan is completed with an invitation to eternal intimacy, described in **Revelation 3:20-22**: *"BEHOLD I STAND AT THE DOOR AND KNOCK, IF ANY MAN HEAR MY VOICE, AND OPEN THE DOOR, I WILL COME INTO HIM, I WILL SUP WITH HIM, AND HE WITH ME TO SIT WITH ME IN MY THRONE, EVEN AS I ALSO OVERCAME AND I AM SET DOWN WITH MY FATHER IN HIS THRONE."*

This promise of dwelling with Christ is the ultimate fulfillment of God's wonderful plan.

These foundational Scriptures stand as pillars of assurance, confirming that salvation is the comprehensive work of God to fully redeem, restore, and rewrite the destiny of His beloved children.

Chapter 7
The Call to Follow

7.1 Come, Follow Me: Jesus' Invitation

"Jesus said, 'Come to me, all you who are weary and burdened, and I will give you rest'" (Matthew 11:28).

This isn't a command—it's an invitation. An open door to a weary soul. "Come" in the midst of brokenness, "follow" in the midst of uncertainty. Jesus doesn't say, "Fix yourself, then come." He says, "Come as you are. I'll give you rest".

3 Truths about Following Jesus:

1. **Rest in Him:** "My yoke is easy and my burden is light" (Matthew 11:30).
2. **Transformation Happens:** "Whoever loses his life for my sake will find it" (Matthew 16:25).
3. **Purpose Found:** "Seek first the kingdom of God... and all these things will be given to you as well" (Matthew 6:33).

"Come, follow me" isn't a formula—it's a relationship. An invitation to walk with the One who sees your weary soul and says, "I have rest." Will you come?

7.2 *Take Up the Cross: Follow Me*

"Jesus said, 'If anyone would come after me, let him deny himself and take up his cross and follow me'" (Matthew 16:24).
The cross wasn't a trendy symbol then—it was brutal, shameful death. Yet Jesus calls you to take it up. Not for masochism, but for transformation. The cross isn't a burden—it's a doorway. To Jesus, to others, to a life beyond yourself.

The Cross Means Radical Surrender:

- **Deny Self, Discover Life:** "Whoever wants to be my disciple must deny themselves" (Matthew 16:24). Self-surrender isn't loss-it's liberation.
- **Join His Suffering, Share His Glory:** "If they persecuted me, they will persecute you" (John 15:20). Jesus didn't promise a bypass-He promised presence.
- **Die to Live, Live to Give:** "Whoever loses his life for my sake will find it" (Matthew 16:25). The cross kills ego, birth's purpose.

3 Cross-Following Realities:

1. **He's with You in the Fire:** The cross doesn't mean pain without purpose. "When you walk through the fire, I will be with you" (Isaiah 43:2).
2. **Others Need Your Scars:** "We who have been through the suffering... will comfort those in any trouble" (2 Corinthians 1:8, 4). Your brokenness + Jesus = a bridge.
3. **Glory Awaits the Surrendered:** "If we suffer with him, we will also be glorified with him" (Romans 8:17).

Practical Cross-Taking:
- Surrender a grudge, choose forgiveness.
- Offer a need, trust God for provision.
- Share Jesus with one person this week. "Take up your cross" isn't a to-do list. It's an upgrade. A path to the abundant life (John 10:10). Jesus didn't stay on the cross. He rose. He invites you to rise with Him.

7.3 Today: The Day of Salvation

"Behold, now is the day of salvation" (2 Corinthians 6:2).
Today. Not tomorrow, not next year, not "someday." *Today* is the moment God says, "I am here. Will you come?".

Why Today?
- **God's Timing is Now:** "The time has come... The kingdom of God has come near" (Mark 1:15).
- **Tomorrow Isn't Promised:** "You do not know what tomorrow will bring... What is your life?" (James 4:14).
- **Jesus Waits at the Door:** "Behold, I stand at the door and knock" (Revelation 3:20).

What Does "Today" Look Like?
- Turn from what's keeping you from God (Repent).
- Trust Jesus paid the price for you (Believe).
- Invite Him in (Surrender).

Now is the time of Favor, now is the day of salvation. This is your *today*. Will you take it?

Chapter 8
Living in Assurance

8.1 Foundations of Our Faith

Faith Faith is not the absence of doubt, but the presence of trust. When we trust in God's goodness and sovereignty, we can have confidence in His plan for our lives. Like Abraham, who "believed God, and it was credited to him as righteousness" (Romans 4:3), we too can experience the joy and peace that come from trusting in God. "Now faith is confidence in what we hope for and assurance about what we do not see" (Hebrews 11:1).

Justification Justification is God's declaration of "not guilty" over our lives. It's not about our performance or achievements, but about Christ's finished work on the cross. When we put our faith in Him, we are declared righteous and holy, just like His Son. As Romans 3:24 says, "and all are justified freely by his grace through the redemption that came by Christ Jesus".

Redemption Redemption is the story of our lives. We're bought back from the slave market of sin and given a new identity as children of God. Like the Israelites escaping slavery in Egypt, we've been set free from bondage and given a new life. As 1 Peter 1:18-19 says, "You were redeemed with the precious blood of Christ, a lamb without blemish or defect".
Jesus paid the price. "You were bought with a price; you are not your own" (1 Corinthians 6:20). Redemption is the story of being bought back from darkness into light. In Luke 15, the lost sheep was redeemed. The lost coin was redeemed. The prodigal son was redeemed. You are the one Jesus seeks, redeems, and restores. He didn't redeem you to leave you broken. He redeemed you to give you a new story, a new purpose, a new family.

8.2 Songs of Salvation

These songs remind us of God's incredible love and grace and can help inspire and deepen our faith.

Classic Hymns

- *Amazing Grace* by John Newton - A timeless classic about God's redeeming love.
- *Come Thou Fount of Every Blessing* by Robert Robinson - A beautiful hymn about God's grace and mercy.
- *All Hail the Power of Jesus' Name* by Edward Perronet - A triumphant song about Jesus' sovereignty.

Contemporary Worship Songs

- *This Is Amazing Grace* by Phil Wickham - A modern classic about God's amazing love.
- *Your Grace Is Enough* by Chris Tomlin - A heartfelt song about trusting in God's grace.
- *Graves Into Gardens* by Elevation Worship - A powerful song about God's redeeming power.
- *Who You Say I Am* by Hillsong Worship - A declaration of our identity in Christ.

8.3 Prayers of Surrender

Prayer: Confession and Belief "Jesus, with my mouth I confess You as Lord. I say it out loud: *You are my Savior, my King, my Life.* With my heart I believe you rose from the dead, you defeated sin, you love me like no one else can. I trust you paid the price for every mistake, every shame, every fear. I receive Your forgiveness, Your peace, Your new life. Thank You for writing my name in Your book, for calling me Yours. Guide me, strengthen me, use me. In Your powerful name, Jesus. Amen.".

Prayer: Surrender and Consecration "Lord, I surrender all to You. Every part, every dream, every breath - it's Yours. Take my life, consecrate it wholly. Let it be a vessel for Your glory, a light for Your path, a love for Your people.
I lay it all at Your feet. Mold me, use me, fill me with Your Spirit. Let my life say 'Jesus, you are enough.'
In the quiet, in the noise, in the mess; *You* are my anchor. I come to stay. In Jesus' name. Amen.".

CONCLUSION:

The Open Door of Grace

The Invitation to Your Own Story

We have journeyed together through the Plan of Salvation from the divine *motive* of God's love in Chapter 1, through the profound *mechanism* of Justification and Sanctification in Chapter 2, and into the *miracle* of Redemption and Regeneration in Chapter 3. We then traced the clear steps of *access* in the Four Spiritual Laws in Chapter 4, and finally, we saw these truths demonstrated in the imperfect, yet powerful, narrative of a life catapulted by God's grace in Chapter 5. The core lesson woven throughout every chapter is simple: God's provision is complete, and His invitation is personal.

My life, marked by hidden struggles in childhood devotion and later, the fearful, trembling prayer at my mother's bedside, is proof that grace works not just in grand moments, but in the gritty reality of everyday life. The transformation from running away from chores to achieving excellence through a *secret command*, and from needing prayer to actively becoming an intercessor for others was powered entirely by the Holy Spirit. This power is not unique to me; it is the inheritance of every person who accepts the gift of salvation.

BIBLIOGRAPHY

This list includes theological works and resources referenced for the doctrinal sections of this book.

- Bright, Bill. *The Four Spiritual Laws.* Orlando: Cru, 1952.
- Packer, J. I. *Knowing God.* Downers Grove, IL: InterVarsity Press, 1973.
- Radmacher, Earl D. *Salvation (Theological Studies).* Portland: Western Seminary Press, 1978.
- **Kennedy, D. James. *Evangelism Explosion.* Tyndale House Publishers, 1970.**

The Holy Bible, New International Version (NIV). Zondervan.

Song:
Inspirations on Salvation

- *Sing with me Redemption coming praise the Lord.*
- *Redeemed when my burden of sin was high.*
- *Burdens are lifted at Calvary.*
- *I know the Lord will make a way for me.*
- *Rescue the perishing.*
- *Amazing Grace.*
- *Come into my Heart Lord Jesus.*
- *Calvary's Cross I shall never forget.*
- *When I survey the wondrous Cross.*

END NOTES

The following notes provide specific sources and scriptural citations for the theological concepts explored in this book.

Chapter 1
Introduction: The Call to Redemption

- **Romans 3:23 (NIV):** "For all have sinned and fall short of the glory of God."
- **John 3:16 (NIV):** "For God so loved the world that he gave his one and only Son, that whoever believes in him shall not perish but have eternal
  - life."

Chapter 2
Defining Salvation: Past, Present, and Future

- Earl D. Radmacher, *Salvation (Theological Studies)* (Portland: Western Seminary Press, 1978). (Used for the framework of Justification, Sanctification, and Glorification).
- Romans 5:1 (NIV): "Therefore, since we have been justified through faith, we have peace with God through our Lord Jesus Christ."
- Romans 8:30 (NIV): "And those he predestined, he also called; those he called, he also justified; those he justified, he also glorified."
- J. I. Packer, *Knowing God* (Downers Grove, IL: InterVarsity Press, 1973). (Used to define the nature of Sanctification as a process).

Chapter 3
The Workable Plan: Inner Transformation

- John 3:3 (NIV): "Jesus replied, 'Very truly I tell you, no one can see the kingdom of God unless they are born again.'"
- Ezekiel 36:26-27 (NIV): "I will give you a new heart and put a new spirit in you... and cause you to walk in my statutes."
- 2 Corinthians 5:17 (NIV): "Therefore, if anyone is in Christ, the new creation has come: The old has gone, the new is here!"
- Ephesians 1:7 (NIV): "In him we have redemption through his blood, the forgiveness of sins, in accordance with the riches of God's grace."

Chapter 4
The Four Spiritual Laws: A Simple Path to God

- Bill Bright, *The Four Spiritual Laws* (Orlando: Cru, 1952). (Used for the four-point outline).
- Romans 5:8 (NIV): "But God demonstrates his
- own love for us in this: While we were still
- sinners, Christ died for us."
- John 1:12 (NIV): "Yet to all who received him, to those who believed in his name, he gave the right to become children of God."

Chapter 5
My Personal Testimony: A Life Catapulted by Grace

- 2 Corinthians 5:17 (NIV): "Therefore, if anyone is in Christ, the new creation has come: The old has gone, the new is here!" (Used to support the concept of inner transformation and a new destiny).
- Romans 8:13 (NIV): "...if by the Spirit you put to death the misdeeds of the body, you will live." (Used to support the theme of living "after the Spirit" and overcoming freshly desires).
- 1 Corinthians 12:7 (NIV): "Now to each one the manifestation of the Spirit is given for the
- common good." (Used to support the demonstration of the Holy Spirit's power through prayer).
- Hebrews 4:16 (NIV): "Let us then approach
- God's throne of grace with confidence, so that we may receive mercy and find grace to help us in our time of need." (Used to support the Son's wisdom about coming to God as you are).
- 1 Peter 5:7 (NIV): "Cast all your anxiety on him because he cares for you." (Used to support turning fear and worry into prayer).

Chapter 6
The Divine Verdict: Foundational Scriptures of Salvation

- St. John 3:16 (NIV): "For God so loved the world that he gave his one and only Son, that whoever believes in him shall not perish but have eternal life."
- Ephesians 2:8-9 (NIV): "For it is by grace you have been saved, through faith and this is not from yourselves, it is the gift of

God not by works, so that no one can boast."

- Romans 10:9-10 (NIV): "That if you shall confess with your mouth the Lord Jesus and shall believe in your heart that God raised him from the dead, you shall be saved. For with the heart man believeth unto righteousness; and with the mouth confession is made unto salvation."
- Acts 4:12 (NIV): "Salvation is found in no other, for there is no other name under heaven given to mankind by which we must be saved."
- Romans 6:23 (NIV): "For the wages of sin is death but the gift of God is eternal life in Christ Jesus our Lord."
- Ephesians 1:7 (NIV): "In him we have redemption through his blood, the forgiveness of sins, according to the richness of his grace."
- 1 Peter 1:18-20 (NIV): "Forasmuch as you know we were not redeemed by corruptible things, as silver and gold... but with the precious blood of Christ, as of a lamb without blemish and without spot, who was ordained before the foundation of the world, but was manifest in this last time for you."
- Romans 4:7 (NIV): "Blessed are they whose iniquities are forgiven and whose sins are covered."
- St. John 1:12 (NIV): "As many as received him, to them he gave the right to become children of God, even to those who believe in his name."
- Revelation 3:20-22 (NIV): "behold I stand at the door and knock, if any man hear my voice, and open the door, I will come into him, I will sup with him, and he with me to sit with me in his throne, even as I also overcame and I am set down with my father in his throne."

<h1 style="text-align:center">Chapter   7</h1>
<h2 style="text-align:center">The Call to Follow</h2>

- Matthew 11:28 (NIV): "Come to me, all you who are weary and burdened, and I will give you rest."
- Matthew 11:30 (NIV): "For my yoke is easy and my burden is light."
- Matthew 16:24 (NIV): "Then Jesus said to his disciples, 'Whoever wants to be my disciple must deny themselves and take up their cross and follow me.'"
- John 15:20 (NIV): "Remember what I told you: 'A servant is not

greater than his master.' If they persecuted me, they would persecute you also."
- Isaiah 43:2 (NIV): "When you pass through the waters, I will be with you... When you walk through the fire, you will not be burned; the flames will not set you ablaze."
- 2 Corinthians 6:2 (NIV): "I tell you, now is the time of God's Favor, now is the day of salvation."

Chapter 8
Living in Assurance

- Hebrews 11:1 (NIV): "Now faith is confidence in what we hope for and assurance about what we do not see."
- Romans 3:24 (NIV): "and all are justified freely by his grace through the redemption that came by Christ Jesus."
- Romans 4:3 (NIV): "What does Scripture say? 'Abraham believed God, and it was credited to him as righteousness.'"
- 1 Corinthians 6:20 (NIV): "you were bought at a price. Therefore, honour God with your bodies."
- 1 Peter 1:18-19 (NIV): "For you know that it was not with perishable things such as silver or gold that you were redeemed... but with the precious blood of Christ, a lamb without blemish or defect."

CONTINUING WORK

Remember that salvation is dynamic. It is not just about the moment you were justified (past tense), but about the continuous, beautiful process of sanctification (present tense). The moment you accepted Christ; you were given the power to live after the Spirit. God has made you holy and set you apart, and now you have the privilege of walking out that new identity daily.

If you have already received Jesus Christ, this book serves as a powerful reminder: you are redeemed, you are free, and you are called to walk in a state of growing holiness. If you are still searching for that missing piece of meaning, the Plan of Salvation is the map to your spiritual home. The door is open; the price has been paid.

The greatest adventure is the one you live in Christ.

May your life, too, be a continuing testimony, profoundly and undeniably catapulted by God's grace.

ABOUT THE AUTHOR

Residing in Naples, Florida, Marion P. McKenzie is a teacher, Pastor, and chaplain at Upper Room Evangelistic Ministries in Ft. Lauderdale, Florida.

Born in Mint Road, Grange Hill, Westmoreland, Jamaica, she is the second of seven children. She holds extensive teaching experience, having trained at Bethlehem Teachers' College and taught at various institutions in Jamaica and the International College of the Cayman Islands. She later lectured at her alma mater, Bethlehem Teachers' College. She has pursued higher education at International Seminary, Sure Foundation College, and Cambridge College in London, England.

Catapulted by God's Grace is a testament to her faith journey, particularly her belief that her life has been profoundly and undeniably "Being propelled by God's grace".

My testimonials

I consider my life to be a miraculous journey, one where I have been blessed to travel the globe with a singular purpose: to experience the boundless beauty of God's creation. My travels have been more than just vacations; they have been a pilgrimage of discovery.

I have traversed the earth by every means possible, soaring through the air, crossing oceans on majestic ships, and rattling across continents on trains and buses. My path has taken me from the familiar landscapes of the United States to the historic depths of Europe and the vibrant cultures of Asia. I remember walking the streets of Germany and standing beneath the towering iron lattice of the Eiffel Tower in Paris, feeling small amidst the vastness of the world.

Among my most profound memories are those from the northern wilderness. Standing on the deck of a ship in Alaska, I was awestruck by the sheer power of nature. Facing those tall, majestic mountains and watching the white glaciers meet the sea was a captivating sight that I will carry with me forever.

With great joy, I recall the warmth of the Caribbean during my years as a teacher in the Cayman Islands. There, I had the unique opportunity to explore the depths of God's underwater world aboard a submarine, gazing in wonder at the life teeming beneath the surface of the ports. From the mountain peaks to the ocean floor, I have toured the world, and I remain amazed by the glory of it all.

LOVE

JOY

FREEDOM

GLORIFICATION

SPIRIT

PEACE

GOD'S MERCY

HOLINESS